CHRISTMAS CAROLS

Christmas Carols

Galahad Books
New York

Published in 1989 by

Galahad Books
A division of LDAP, Inc.
166 Fifth Avenue
New York, NY 10010

Published by arrangement with W.S. Konecky Associates.

Book design by Abe Lerner.

Illustration on front of jacket. Grandma Moses: *White Christmas.* Collection of Mr. &
Mrs. Irving Berlin. Copyright © 1979, Grandma Moses Properties Co., New York.

Anna Mary Robertson Moses (1860–1961) began painting in old age and became
internationally famous as "Grandma" Moses. She is associated with the Christmas
holidays because of her predilection for cheery winter scenes.

ISBN 0-88365-744-9

CONTENTS

Arranged Alphabetically

INTRODUCTION

Over the centuries a body of songs has grown to become a hallmark of the Christmas season. The earliest carols date back to the 1400's; the first printed sample is the *Boar's Head Carol,* reproduced in these pages. The singing of carols has always been associated with dancing, and as such they are lively and jolly in character. Perhaps their continuing appeal lies in their high spirited approach to solemn matters. So we have felt no hesitation in bringing together traditional carols such as *Deck The Halls* and *God Rest You Merry, Gentlemen* with the contemporary favorite *Rudolph the Red-Nosed Reindeer.*

Carols are meant to be played, sung and enjoyed. This book's sewn binding allows pages to open easily and lie flat. All songs are presented in easy-to-play full-sounding arrangements within standard vocal ranges. Guitar chords accompany the music and traditional woodcuts and engravings set off the text.

It is our hope that *The Family Book Of Christmas Carols* will bring you all the joy of the Christmas season and be part of your family's Christmas celebration for many years to come.

—THE PUBLISHER

On Christmas Night

ANONYMOUS

ANONYMOUS

FROM: INTERNATIONAL CHRISTMAS by Ada Richter
© 1966 Theodore Presser Company
Reprinted By Permission Of The Publisher

9

News of our mer - ci - ful King's birth.
All for to gain our lib - er - ty.

3. All out of darkness we have light,
   Which made the angels sing this night;
   All out of darkness we have light,
   Which made the angels sing this night;
   "Glory to God and peace to men,
   Now and forevermore, Amen.

Up On The Housetop

BENJAMIN R. HANBY   BENJAMIN R. HANBY

Allegretto

1. Up on the house-top rein-deer pause, Out jumps good old San-ta Claus;

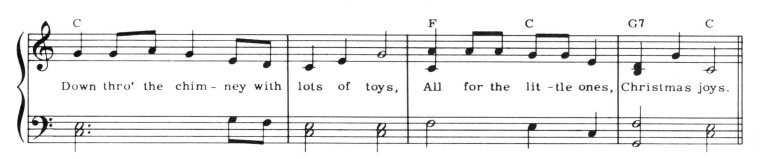

Down thro' the chim-ney with lots of toys, All for the lit-tle ones, Christmas joys.

Chorus

Ho, ho, ho! Who would-n't go! Ho, ho, ho! Who would-n't go!

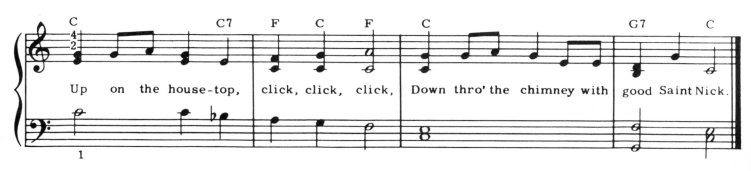

Up on the house-top, click, click, click, Down thro' the chimney with good Saint Nick.

2. First comes the stocking of little Nell,
Oh, dear Santa, fill it well;
Give her a dollie that laughs and cries,
One that will open and shut her eyes.
Chorus

3. Next comes the stocking of little Will,
Oh, just see what a glorious fill!
Here is a hammer and a lots of tacks,
Also a ball and whip that cracks.
Chorus

FROM: INTERNATIONAL CHRISTMAS by Ada Richter
© 1966 Theodore Presser Company
Reprinted By Permission Of The Publisher

The Twelve Days of Christmas

ANONYMOUS

ANONYMOUS

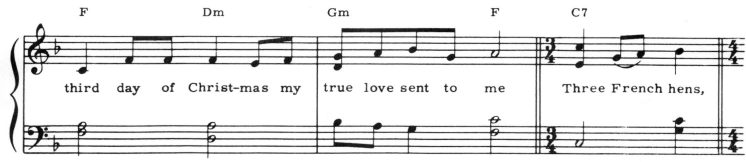

FROM: INTERNATIONAL CHRISTMAS by Ada Richter
© 1966 Theodore Presser Company
Reprinted By Permission Of The Publisher

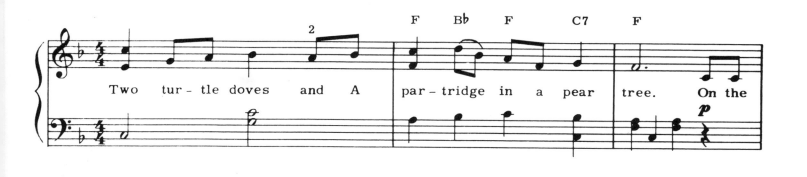

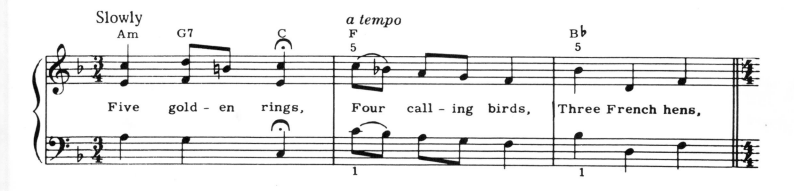

13

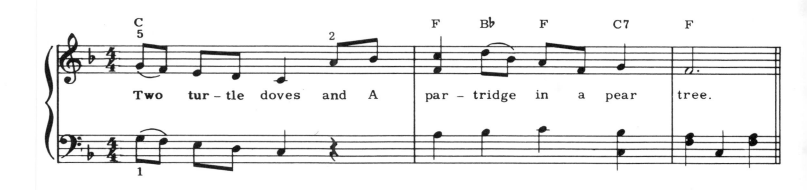

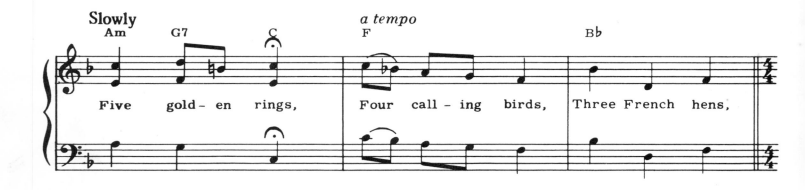

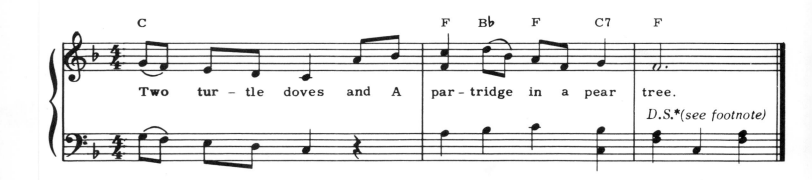

*Continue ad libitum, as follows:

On the seventh day	Seven swans a-swimming, (*Measure 33 two times*)
On the eighth day	Eight maids a-milking, (*Measure 33 three times*)
On the ninth day	Nine ladies dancing, (*Measure 33 four times*)
On the tenth day	Ten lords a-leaping, (*Measure 33 five times*)
On the eleventh day	Eleven pipers piping, (*Measure 33 six times*)
On the twelfth day	Twelve drummers drumming, (*Measure 33 seven times*)

Rudolph The Red-Nosed Reindeer

JOHNNY MARKS

JOHNNY MARKS

Lightly

Verse: *(ad lib)*

Dm7   Em   G9   C   Dm7   Em

You know Dash- er and Danc- er and Pranc- er and Vix- en, Com- et and Cu- pid and

colla voce
mf

G9   C   Am   E7/B   Am/C   Am7   D9   G7

Don- ner and Blitz- en, but do you re - call the most fa - mous rein- deer of all.

Refrain: *(a tempo)*

C   C/E F#dim/Eb G7

Ru- dolph, the red - nosed rein - deer had a ver - y shin - y nose,

mp

and if you ev - er saw it, you would e - ven say it glows.

All of the oth - er rein - deer used to laugh and call him names,

they nev - er let poor Ru - dolph join in an - y rein - deer games.

Then one fog - gy Christ - mas Eve, San - ta came to say,

mp a tempo

The Coventry Carol

ROBERT CROO, 1534

ANONYMOUS, 1591

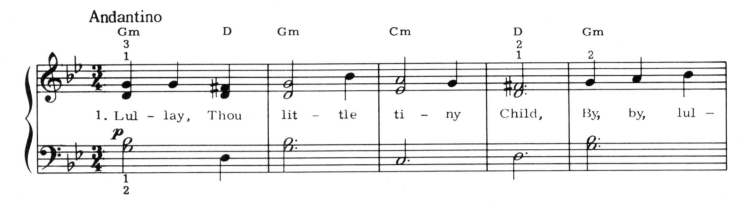

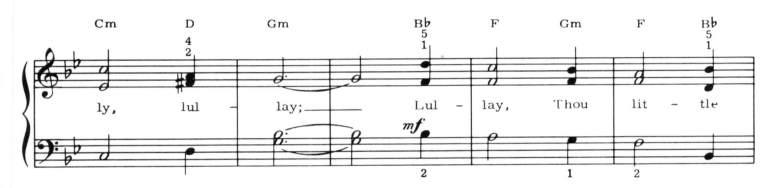

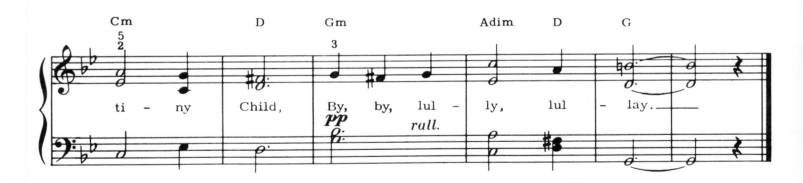

2. O sisters, too, how may we do
   For to preserve this day;
   This poor Youngling for whom we sing,
   By, by, lully, lullay?

3. Herod the king, in his raging,
   Charged he hath this day,
   His men of might in his own sight
   All children young to slay.

4. Then woe is me, poor Child, for Thee,
   And ever morn and day;
   For Thy parting nor say nor sing,
   By, by, lully, lullay.

FROM: INTERNATIONAL CHRISTMAS by Ada Richter
© 1966 Theodore Presser Company
Reprinted By Permission Of The Publisher

O Come, O Come, Emmanuel

LATIN: ANONYMOUS, c.9TH CENTURY
ENGLISH: JOHN M. NEALE, 1851
(1818–1866)

ANONYMOUS, 13TH CENTURY
ADAPTED BY THOMAS HELMORE, 1854
(1811–1890)

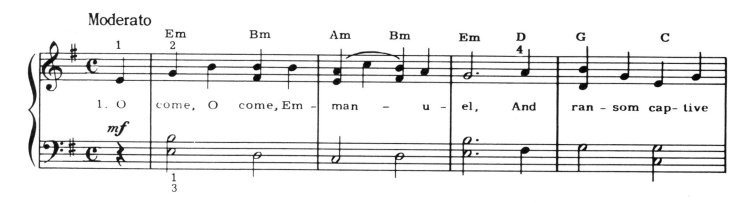

1. O come, O come, Em- man – u – el, And ran – som cap- tive

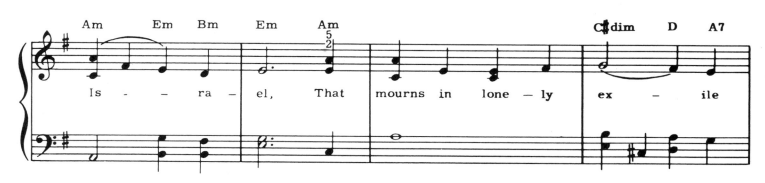

Is – – ra – el, That mourns in lone – ly ex – – ile

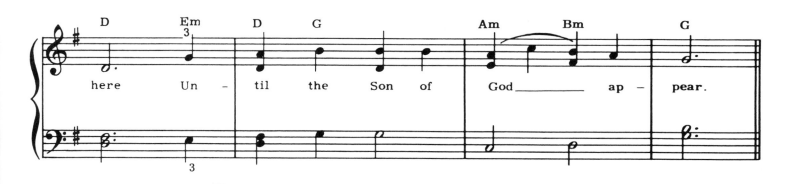

here Un – til the Son of God _____ ap – pear.

Chorus

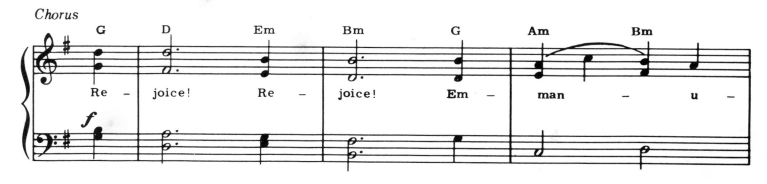

Re – joice! Re – joice! Em – man – u –

el   Shall   come   to   thee,   O   Is — ra —   el.

2. O come, Thou Rod of Jesse, free
   Thine own from Satan's tyranny;
   From depths of hell thy people save,
   And give them vict'ry o'er the grave.
   Chorus

3. O come, Thou Day-Spring, come and cheer
   Our spirits by Thine advent here;
   Disperse the gloomy clouds of night,
   And death's dark shadows put to flight.
   Chorus

4. O come, Thou Key of David, come,
   And open wide our heav'nly home;
   Make safe the way that leads on high,
   And close the path to misery.
   Chorus

5. O come, O come, Thou Lord of might,
   Who to Thy tribes, on Sinai's height,
   In ancient times did'st give the law,
   In cloud, and majesty and awe.
   Chorus

While Shepherds Watched Their Flocks

NAHUM TATE, 1708
(1652–1715)

ARR. FROM GEORGE F. HANDEL, 1728
(1685–1759)

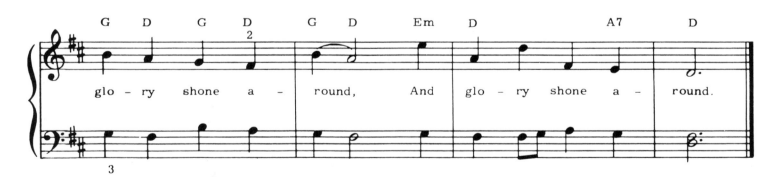

2. "Fear not!" said he for mighty dread.
Had seized their troubled mind,
"Glad tidings of great joy I bring,
To you and all mankind,
To you and all mankind."

3. "To you, in David's town this day,
Is born of David's line,
The Saviour, who is Christ the Lord;
And this shall be the sign,
And this shall be the sign."

4. "The heav'nly Babe you there shall find
To human view displayed,
All meanly wrapped in swathing bands,
And in a manger laid,
And in a manger laid."

5. "All glory be to God on high,
And to the earth be peace:
Good-will henceforth from heaven to men
Begin and never cease,
Begin and never cease!"

Good Christian Men, Rejoice

JOHN M. NEALE, 1853
(1818–1866)

TUNE: IN DULCI JUBILO, 14TH CENTURY

2. Good Christian men, rejoice
With heart, and soul, and voice;
Now ye hear of endless bliss:
Jesus Christ was born for this!
He hath ope'd the heav'nly door,
And man is blessed evermore.
Christ was born for this!
Christ was born for this!

3. Good Christian men, rejoice
With heart, and soul, and voice;
Now ye need not fear the grave:
Jesus Christ was born to save!
Calls you one and calls you all
To gain His everlasting hall.
Christ was born to save!
Christ was born to save!

22

FROM: INTERNATIONAL CHRISTMAS by Ada Richter
© 1966 Theodore Presser Company
Reprinted By Permission Of The Publisher

I Saw Three Ships

ANONYMOUS   ANONYMOUS

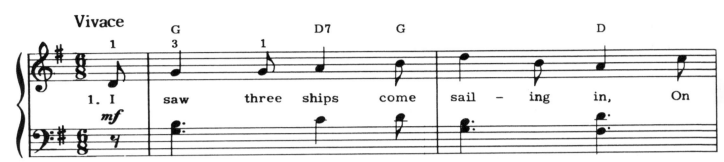

2. And what was in those ships all three,
   On Christmas Day, on Christmas Day?
   And what was in those ships all three,
   On Christmas Day in the morning?

3. The Virgin Mary and Christ were there,
   On Christmas Day, on Christmas Day;
   The Virgin Mary and Christ were there,
   On Christmas Day in the morning.

4. O they sailed into Bethlehem,
   On Christmas Day, on Christmas Day;
   O they sailed into Bethlehem,
   On Christmas Day in the morning.

5. And all the bells on earth shall ring
   On Christmas Day, on Christmas Day;
   And all the bells on earth shall ring
   On Christmas Day in the morning.

6. And all the souls on earth shall sing,
   On Christmas Day, on Christmas Day;
   And all the souls on earth shall sing,
   On Christmas Day in the morning.

7. Then let us all rejoice amain,
   On Christmas Day, on Christmas Day;
   Then let us all rejoice amain,
   On Christmas Day in the morning.

It Came Upon The Midnight Clear

EDMUND H. SEARS, 1846
(1810–1876)

RICHARD S. WILLIS, 1850
(1819–1900)

FROM: INTERNATIONAL CHRISTMAS by Ada Richter
© 1966 Theodore Presser Company
Reprinted By Permission Of The Publisher

2. Still through the cloven skies they come
   With peaceful wings unfurled,
   And still their heavenly music floats
   O'er all the weary world;
   Above its sad and lowly plains
   They bend on hovering wing,
   And ever over its babel sounds
   The blessed angels sing.

3. Yet with the woes of sin and strife
   The world has suffered long;
   Beneath the heavenly strain have rolled
   Two thousand years of wrong;
   And man, at war with man, hears not
   The tidings which they bring;
   O hush the noise, ye men of strife,
   And hear the angels sing.

4. O ye, beneath life's crushing load,
   Whose forms are bending low,
   Who toil along the climbing way
   With painful steps and slow;
   Look now! for glad and golden hours
   Come swiftly on the wing;
   O rest beside the weary road
   And hear the angels sing.

5. For lo! the days are hastening on,
   By prophets seen of old,
   When with the ever-circling years
   Shall come the time foretold,
   When peace shall over all the earth
   Its ancient splendors fling,
   And the whole world give back the song
   Which now the angels sing.

Good King Wenceslas

JOHN M. NEALE, 1853
(1818–1866)

ANONYMOUS, 1582

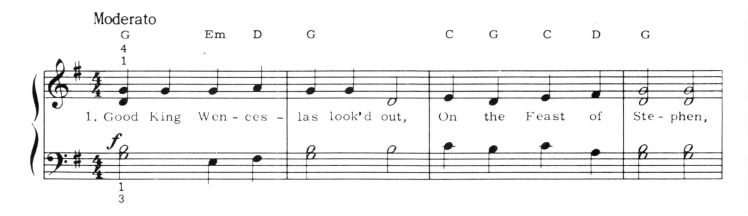

1. Good King Wen-ces-las look'd out, On the Feast of Ste-phen,

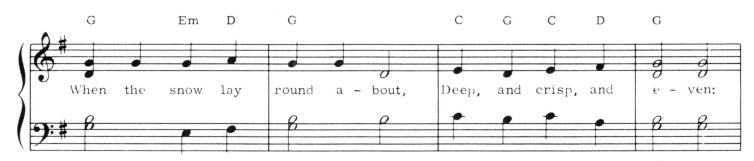

When the snow lay round a-bout, Deep, and crisp, and e-ven:

Bright-ly shone the moon that night, Though the frost was cru-el,

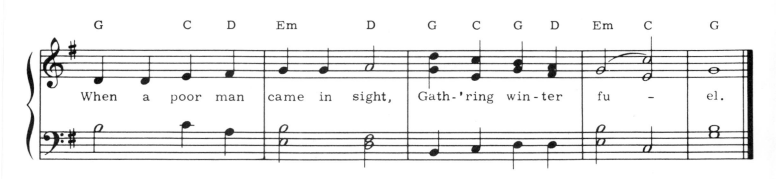

When a poor man came in sight, Gath-'ring win-ter fu - el.

FROM: INTERNATIONAL CHRISTMAS by Ada Richter
© 1966 Theodore Presser Company
Reprinted By Permission Of The Publisher

2. "Hither, page, and stand by me,
      If thou know'st it, telling,
   Yonder peasant, who is he?
      Where and what his dwelling?"
   "Sire, he lives a good league hence,
      Underneath the mountain;
   Right against the forest fence,
      By Saint Agnes' fountain."

3. "Bring me flesh, and bring me wine,
      Bring me pine-logs hither:
   Thou and I will see him dine,
      When we bear them thither."
   Page and monarch, forth they went,
      Forth they went together;
   Through the rude wind's wild lament
      And the bitter weather.

4. "Sire, the night is darker now,
      And the wind blows stronger;
   Fails my heart, I know not how;
      I can go no longer."
   "Mark my footsteps, good my page;
      Tread thou in them boldly:
   Thou shalt find the winter's rage
      Freeze thy blood less coldly."

5. In his master's steps he trod,
      Where the snow lay dinted;
   Heat was in the very sod
      Which the Saint had printed.
   Therefore, Christian men, be sure,
      Wealth or rank possessing,
   Ye who now will bless the poor,
      Shall yourselves find blessing.

"ON CHRISTMAS DAY IN THE MORNING"
WITH THE COMPLIMENTS OF ST NICHOLAS

Joy To The World

ISAAC WATTS, 1719
(1674–1748)

LOWELL MASON, 1839
(1792–1872)

3. No more let sins and sorrows grow,
   Nor thorns infest the ground;
   He comes to make His blessings flow
   Far as the curse is found,
   Far as the curse is found,
   Far as, far as the curse is found.

4. He rules the world with truth and grace,
   And makes the nations prove
   The glories of His righteousness,
   And wonders of His love,
   And wonders of His love,
   And wonders, wonders of His love.

FROM: INTERNATIONAL CHRISTMAS by Ada Richter
© 1966 Theodore Presser Company
Reprinted By Permission Of The Publisher

Angels We Have Heard On High

FRENCH: ANONYMOUS
ENGLISH: ANONYMOUS

ANONYMOUS, 1855

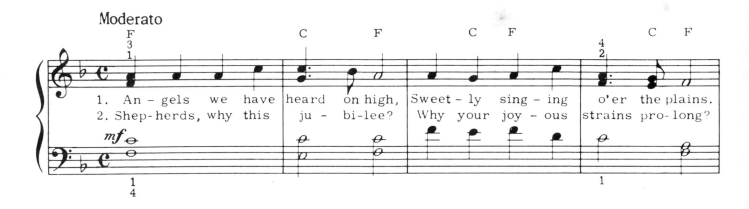

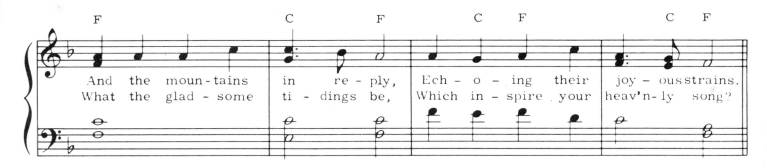

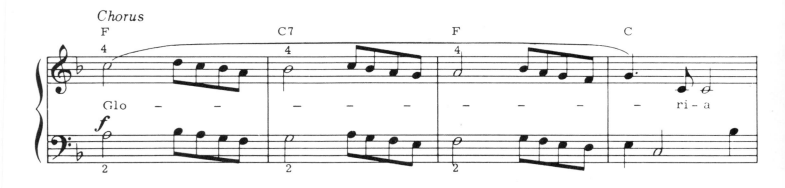

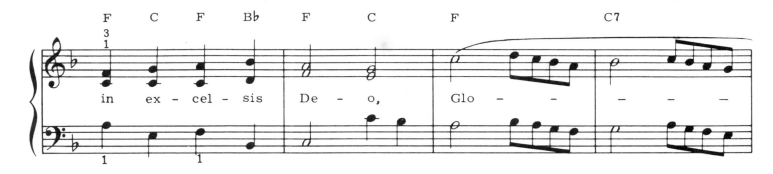

FROM: INTERNATIONAL CHRISTMAS by Ada Richter
© 1966 Theodore Presser Company
Reprinted By Permission Of The Publisher

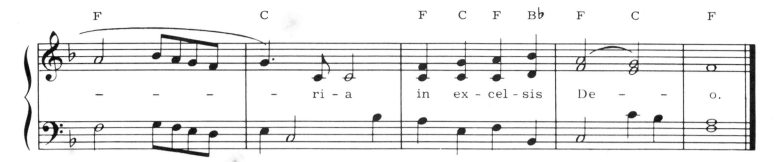

- - - - ri - a in ex - cel - sis De - o.

3. Come, to Bethlehem, and see
   Him whose birth the angels sing;
   Come, adore on bended knee,
   Christ the Lord, the new-born King.
   Chorus

4. See Him in the manger laid,
   Whom the choirs of angels praise;
   Mary, Joseph lend your aid,
   While our hearts in love we raise.
   Chorus

O Come, All Ye Faithful

LATIN: ANONYMOUS, 18TH CENTURY
ENGLISH: FREDERICK OAKELEY, 1852
(1802–1880)

ATTRIBUTED TO JOHN F. WADE, c.1740
(1711–1786)

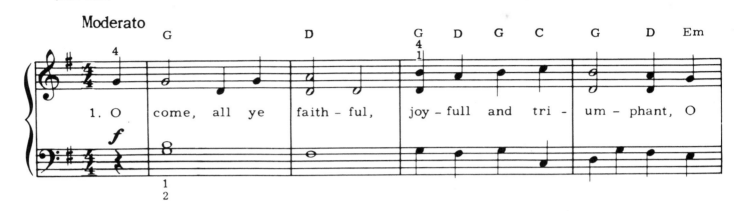

Moderato

1. O come, all ye faith-ful, joy-full and tri-um-phant, O

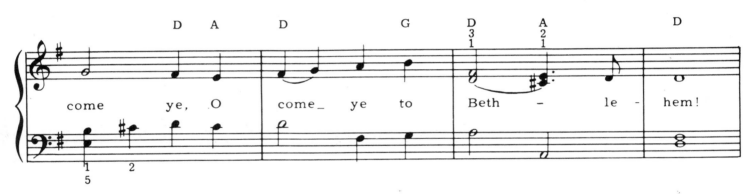

come ye, O come ye to Beth - le - hem!

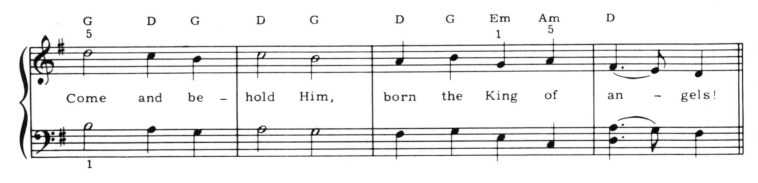

Come and be-hold Him, born the King of an - gels!

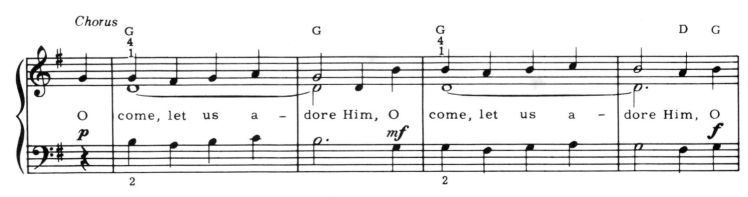

Chorus

O come, let us a - dore Him, O come, let us a - dore Him, O

32

FROM: INTERNATIONAL CHRISTMAS by Ada Richter
© 1966 Theodore Presser Company
Reprinted By Permission Of The Publisher

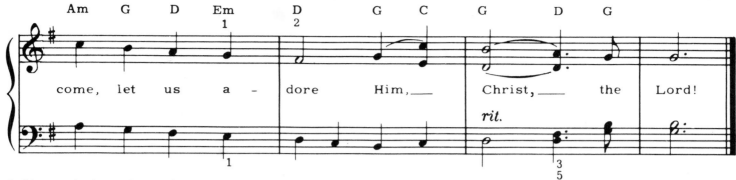

come, let us a - dore Him,___ Christ,___ the Lord!

rit.

2. Sing, choirs of angels, sing in exultation,
   O sing, all ye citizens of heav'n above !
   Glory to God, all glory in the highest !
   Chorus

3. Yea, Lord, we greet Thee, born this happy morning,
   Jesus, to Thee be all glory giv'n;
   Word of the Father, now in flesh appearing !
   Chorus

Christmas Bell Carol

ENGLISH: GEORGE W. ANTHONY, 1966

ANONYMOUS

FROM: INTERNATIONAL CHRISTMAS by Ada Richter
© 1966 Theodore Presser Company
Reprinted By Permission Of The Publisher

Rockin' Around The Christmas Tree

JOHNNY MARKS

JOHNNY MARKS

A Child This Day Is Born

ANONYMOUS, 1833

ANONYMOUS, 1833

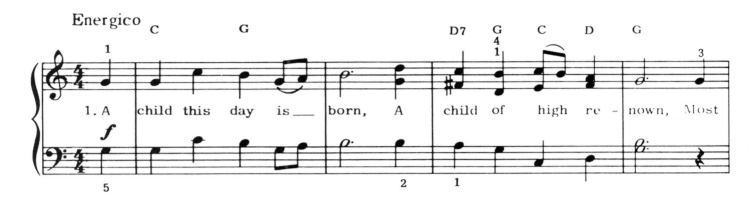

2. These tidings shepherds heard,
   In field watching their fold,
   Were by an angel unto them
   That night revealed and told.

3. To whom the angel spoke,
   Saying, "Be not afraid;
   Be glad, poor silly shepherds,
   Why are you so dismayed?

4. For lo! I bring you tidings
   Of gladness and of mirth,
   Which cometh to all people by
   This holy infant's birth."

5. And as the angel told them,
   So to them did appear;
   They found the young child, Jesus Christ
   With Mary, his mother dear.

FROM: INTERNATIONAL CHRISTMAS by Ada Richter
© 1966 Theodore Presser Company
Reprinted By Permission Of The Publisher

Lo, How A Rose E'er Blooming

GERMAN: ANONYMOUS
ENGLISH: THEODORE BAKER, 1894
(1851–1934)

ANONYMOUS, 1599

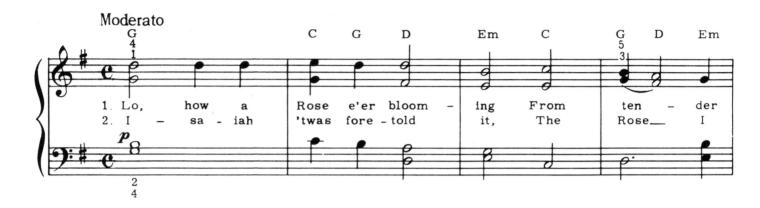

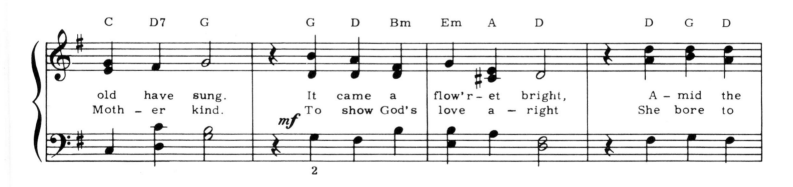

Lyrics:

1. Lo, how a Rose e'er bloom-ing From ten-der Stem hath sprung! Of Jes-se's lin-eage com-ing As men of old have sung. It came a flow'r-et bright, A-mid the cold of win-ter, When half spent was the night.

2. I-sa-iah 'twas fore-told it, The Rose I have in mind, With Ma-ry we be-hold it, The Vir-gin Moth-er kind. To show God's love a-right She bore to men a Sav-iour, When half spent was the night.

Deck The Hall

ANONYMOUS, 1881

WELSH TUNE: ANONYMOUS, 1784

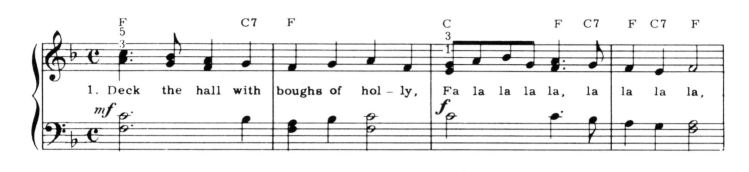

1. Deck the hall with boughs of hol—ly, Fa la la la la, la la la la,

'Tis the sea—son to be jol—ly, Fa la la la la, la la la la,

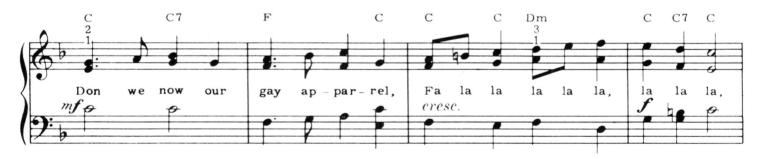

Don we now our gay ap—par—rel, Fa la la la la la, la la la,

Troll the an—cient Christmas car—ol, Fa la la la la, la la la la.

2. See the blazing Yule before us,
   Fa la la la la, la la la la,
   Strike the harp and join the chorus,
   Fa la la la la, la la la la,
   Follow me in merry measure,
   Fa la la la la la,la la la,
   While I tell of Christmas treasure,
   Fa la la la la, la la la la.

3. Fast away the old year passes,
   Fa la la la la, la la la la,
   Hail the new! ye lads and lasses,
   Fa la la la la, la la la la,
   Sing we joyous all together,
   Fa la la la la la,la la la,
   Heedless of the wind and weather,
   Fa la la la la, la la la la.

FROM: INTERNATIONAL CHRISTMAS by Ada Richter
© 1966 Theodore Presser Company
Reprinted By Permission Of The Publisher

Go Tell It On The Mountain

ANONYMOUS

ANONYMOUS

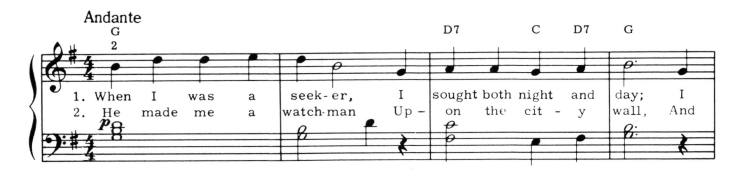

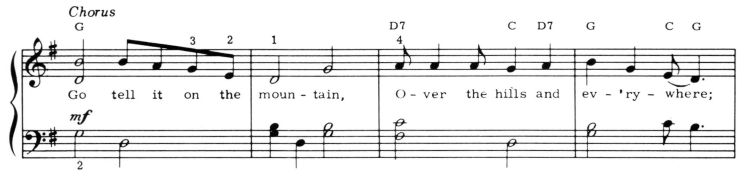

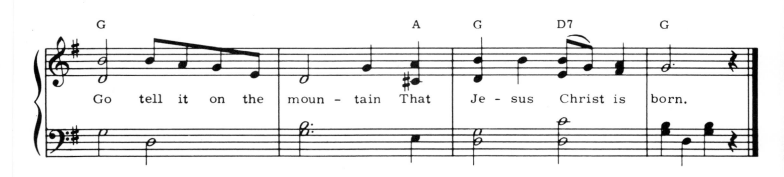

The Seven Joys Of Mary

ANONYMOUS

ANONYMOUS

Allegretto

1. The first good joy that Ma-ry had, It was the joy of one;__ To

see the bless—ed Je-sus Christ, When He was first her Son.__

Chorus

When He was first her Son, Good Lord; And hap—py may we be;__ Praise

Fa-ther, Son, and Ho-ly Ghost, To all e-ter-ni—ty.__

FROM: INTERNATIONAL CHRISTMAS by Ada Richter
© 1966 Theodore Presser Company
Reprinted By Permission Of The Publisher

2. The next good joy that Mary had,
   It was the joy of two;
   To see her own Son Jesus Christ,
   Making the lame to go.
     Chorus : Making the lame to go,
        Good Lord; *etc.*

3. The next good joy that Mary had,
   It was the joy of three;
   To see her own Son Jesus Christ,
   Making the blind to see.
     Chorus : Making the blind to see,
        Good Lord; *etc.*

4. The next good joy that Mary had,
   It was the joy of four;
   To see her own Son Jesus Christ,
   Reading the Bible o'er.
     Chorus : Reading the Bible o'er,
        Good Lord; *etc.*

5. The next good joy that Mary had,
   It was the joy of five;
   To see her own Son Jesus Christ,
   Raising the dead to life.
     Chorus : Raising the dead to life,
        Good Lord; *etc.*

6. The next good joy that Mary had,
   It was the joy of six,
   To see her own Son Jesus Christ,
   Upon the Crucifix,
     Chorus : Upon the Crucifix,
        Good Lord; *etc.*

7. The next good joy that Mary had,
   It was the joy of seven,
   To see her own Son Jesus Christ,
   Ascending into heav'n.
     Chorus : Ascending into heav'n,
        Good Lord; *etc.*

What Child Is This?

WILLIAM C. DIX, c.1865
(1837–1898)

TUNE: GREENSLEEVES, 16TH CENTURY

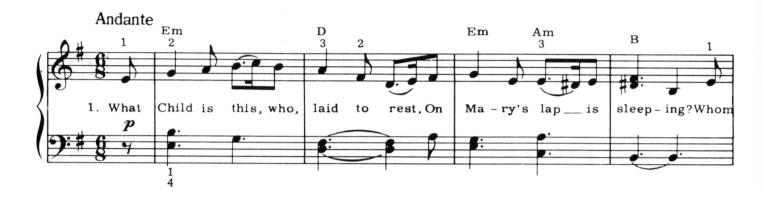

2. **Why lies He in such mean estate**
   Where ox and ass are feeding?
   Good Christian, fear: for sinners here
   The silent Word is pleading.
   Chorus

3. **So bring Him incense, gold and myrrh,**
   Come, peasant, King to own Him;
   The King of kings salvation brings,
   Let loving hearts enthrone Him.
   Chorus

FROM: INTERNATIONAL CHRISTMAS by Ada Richter
© 1966 Theodore Presser Company
Reprinted By Permission Of The Publisher

Bring A Torch, Jeannette, Isabella

FRENCH: EMILE BLEMONT
ENGLISH: E. CUTHBERT NUNN
(1868–1914)

ANONYMOUS, 17TH CENTURY

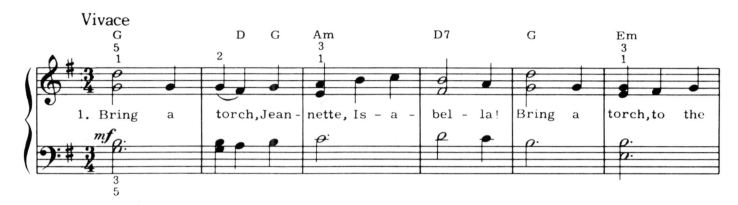

1. Bring a torch, Jean-nette, Is-a-bel-la! Bring a torch, to the

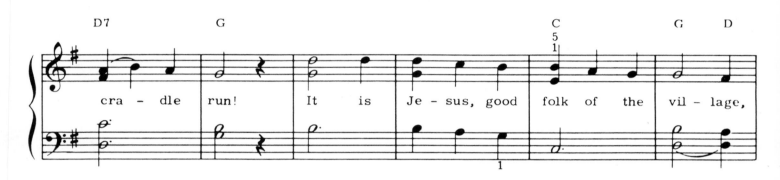

cra-dle run! It is Je-sus, good folk of the vil-lage,

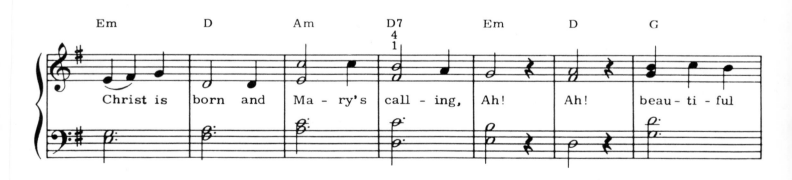

Christ is born and Ma-ry's call-ing, Ah! Ah! beau-ti-ful

is the moth-er; Ah! Ah! beau-ti-ful is her Son.

48

FROM: INTERNATIONAL CHRISTMAS by Ada Richter
© 1966 Theodore Presser Company
Reprinted By Permission Of The Publisher

2. It is **wrong when** the Child is sleeping,
   It is **wrong to talk** so loud.
   Silence, all, as you gather around,
   Lest **your** noise should waken Jesus:
   Hush! **Hush!** see how fast He slumbers;
   Hush! **Hush!** see how fast He sleeps!

3. Softly to the little stable,
   Softly for a moment come!
   Look and see how charming is Jesus,
   How He is white, His cheeks are rosy!
   Hush! Hush! see how the Child is sleeping;
   Hush! Hush! see how He **smiles** in dreams!

Jingle Bells

JAMES PIERPONT, 1857
(1822–1893)

JAMES PIERPONT, 1857
(1822–1893)

1. Dash-ing thro' the snow In a one-horse o-pen sleigh, As o'er the fields we go, A-laugh-ing all the way; The bells on bob-tail ring, And mak-ing spir-its bright; What fun it is to ride and sing A sleigh-ing song to-night!

Jin - gle Bells!   Jin - gle Bells!   Jin - gle all the

way!   Oh, what fun it   is to ride In a

one - horse o - pen   sleigh!   one - horse o - pen   sleigh!

2. Day or two ago
  I thought I'd take a ride,
  And soon Miss Fanny Bright
  Was seated at my side;
  The horse was lean and lank,
  Misfortune seem'd his lot,
  He got into a drifted bank
  And then we got upsot!
  Chorus

3. Now the ground is white,
  You should go it while you're young,
  So take the girls tonight
  And sing this sleighing song;
  Just get a bob-tailed nag,
  Two-forty for his speed,
  Then hitch him to an open sleigh
  And crack! you'll take the lead.
  Chorus

O Holy Night

FRENCH: CAPPEAU DE ROQUEMAURE
ENGLISH: JOHN S. DWIGHT
(1813–1893)

ADOLPHE ADAM, 1847
(1803–1856)

Here We Come A-Wassailing

ANONYMOUS

ANONYMOUS, 19TH CENTURY

Allegro moderato

1. Now here we come a - was - sail - ing A - mong the leaves so
2. We are not dai - ly beg — gars That beg from door to

green,— It's here we come a - wan-d'ring, So fair___ to be seen:
door,— But we are neigh-bors' chil-dren Whom you have seen be - fore:

Chorus

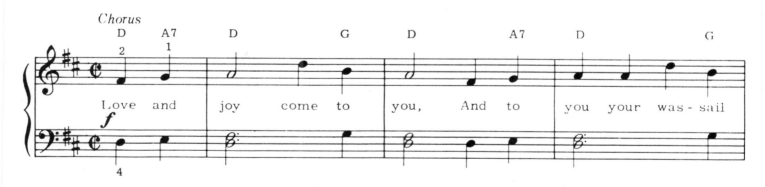

Love and joy come to you, And to you your was-sail

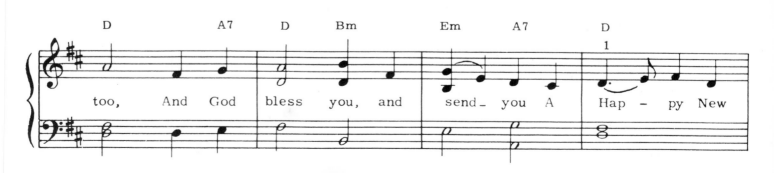

too, And God bless you, and send_ you A Hap — py New

FROM: INTERNATIONAL CHRISTMAS by Ada Richter
© 1966 Theodore Presser Company
Reprinted By Permission Of The Publisher

Year, And God send you A Hap - py New _ Year.

3. Good master and good mistress,
   While you sit by fire,
   Pray think of us poor children
   Who wander in the mire:
   Chorus

4. God bless the master of this house,
   Likewise the mistress too;
   And all the little children
   That round the table go:
   Chorus

Away In A Manger

ANONYMOUS

ANONYMOUS

1. A - way in a man - ger, no crib for His bed, The lit - tle Lord Je - sus laid down His sweet head. The stars in the sky look'd down where He lay, The lit - tle Lord Je - sus, a - sleep on the hay.

2. The cat - tle are low - ing, the Ba - by a - wakes, But lit - tle Lord Je - sus, no cry - ing he makes. I love Thee, Lord Je - sus, look down from the sky, And stay by my cra - dle till morn - ing is nigh.

5 8

FROM: INTERNATIONAL CHRISTMAS by Ada Richter
© 1966 Theodore Presser Company
Reprinted By Permission Of The Publisher

Masters In This Hall

WILLIAM MORRIS, c.1860
(1834–1896)

FRENCH TUNE: ANONYMOUS

Moderato

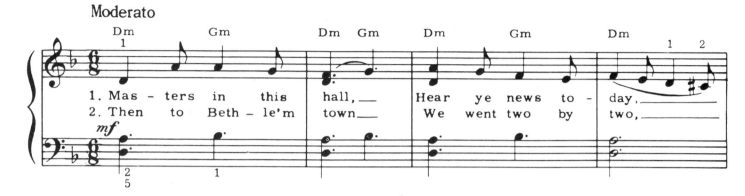

1. Mas - ters in this hall, ___ Hear ye news to - day,
2. Then to Beth - le'm town ___ We went two by two, ___

Brought from o - ver - seas And ev - er you I pray:
In a sor - ry place ___ Heard the ox - en low:

Chorus

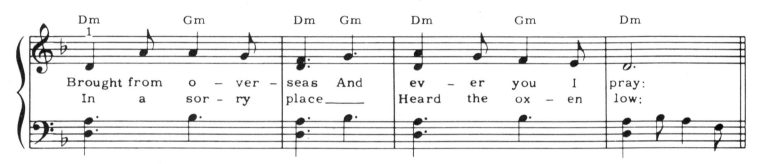

No - well! No - well! No - well! No - well sing we clear! Holp - en
No - well! No - well! No - well! No - well sing we loud! God to -

are all folk on earth, Born is God's Son so dear.
day hath poor folk raised And | cast a-down the proud.

3. Ox and ass Him know,
   Kneeling on their knee,
   Wondrous joy had I
   This little Babe to see:
   Chorus

4. This is Christ, the Lord
   Masters be ye glad!
   Christmas is come in,
   And no folk should be sad!
   Chorus

FROM: INTERNATIONAL CHRISTMAS by Ada Richter
© 1966 Theodore Presser Company
Reprinted By Permission Of The Publisher

59

Silent Night, Holy Night

GERMAN: JOSEPH MOHR, 1818
(1792–1848)
ENGLISH: ANONYMOUS, 1871

FRANZ X. GRUBER, 1818
(1787–1863)

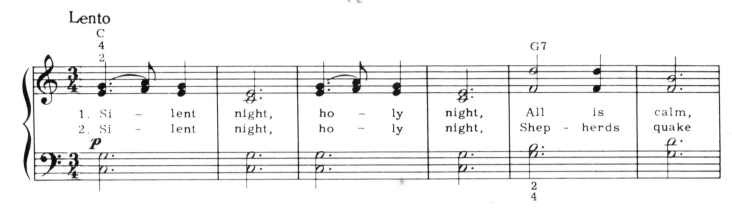

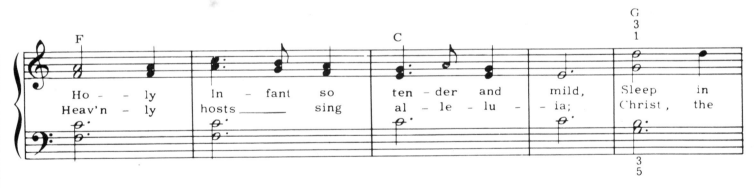

3. Silent night, holy night,
Son of God, love's pure light
Radiant beams from Thy holy face,
With the dawn of redeeming grace,
Jesus, Lord, at Thy birth,
Jesus, Lord, at Thy birth.

4. Silent night, holy night,
Wondrous star, lend thy light,
With the angels let us sing,
Alleluia to our King,
Christ, the Saviour, is born,
Christ, the Saviour, is born.

FROM: INTERNATIONAL CHRISTMAS by Ada Richter
© 1966 Theodore Presser Company
Reprinted By Permission Of The Publisher

Jolly Old Saint Nicholas

ANONYMOUS

ANONYMOUS

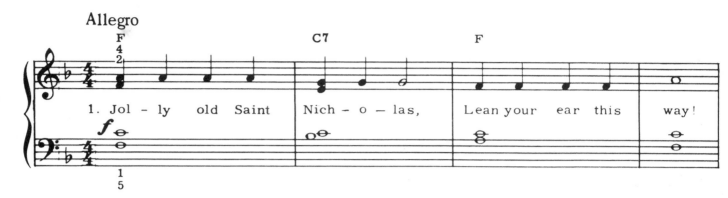

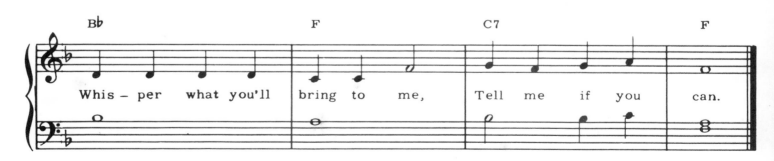

2. When the clock is striking twelve,
When I'm fast asleep,
Down the chimney broad and black,
With your pack you'll creep;
All the stockings you will find
Hanging in a row;
Mine will be the shortest one,
You'll be sure to know.

3. Johnny wants a pair of skates,
Susy wants a sled;
Nellie wants a picture book,
Yellow, blue and red;
Now I think I'll leave to you
What to give the rest;
Choose for me, dear Santa Claus,
You will know the best.

6 2

FROM: INTERNATIONAL CHRISTMAS by Ada Richter
© 1966 Theodore Presser Company
Reprinted By Permission Of The Publisher

Hark! The Herald Angels Sing

CHARLES WESLEY, 1739
(1707–1788)
ALTERED BY GEORGE WHITEFIELD, 1753
(1714–1770)

FELIX MENDELSSOHN, 1840
(1809–1847)
ADAPTED BY WILLIAM H. CUMMINGS, 1840
(1831–1915)

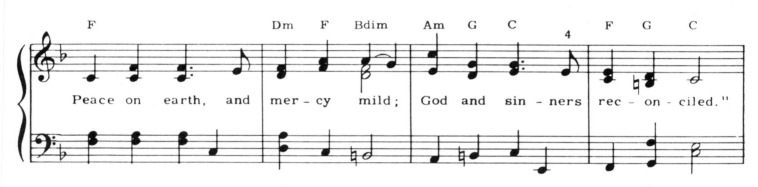

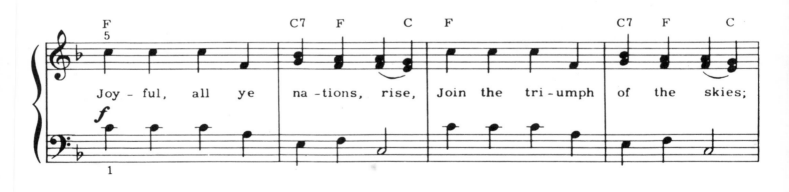

FROM: INTERNATIONAL CHRISTMAS by Ada Richter
© 1966 Theodore Presser Company
Reprinted By Permission Of The Publisher

Hark! the her-ald an-gels sing, "Glo-ry__ to the new-born King."

2. Christ, by highest heaven adored,
   Christ, the everlasting Lord:
   Long desired, behold Him come,
   Finding here His humble home.
   Veiled in flesh the God-head see,
   Hail th'incarnate Deity!
   Pleased as man with men to dwell,
   Jesus our Immanuel.
   Hark! the herald angels sing,
   "Glory to the new-born King."

3. Hail the heav'n-born Prince of Peace!
   Hail the Sun of righteousness!
   Light and life to all He brings,
   Risen with healing in His wings.
   Mild He lays His glory by,
   Born that man no more may die,
   Born to raise the sons of earth,
   Born to give them second birth.
   Hark! the herald angels sing,
   "Glory to the new-born King."

March Of The Kings

FRENCH: ANONYMOUS

ENGLISH: GEORGE W. ANTHONY, 1966

ANONYMOUS, 13TH CENTURY

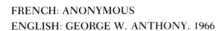

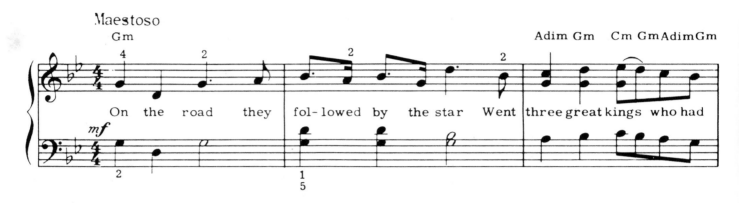

On the road they fol-lowed by the star Went three great kings who had

trav-elled far;__ Their__ gifts to bring the new-born in-fant King, Whose

fame had called them from lands a - far. Their gifts of gold, frank-in-

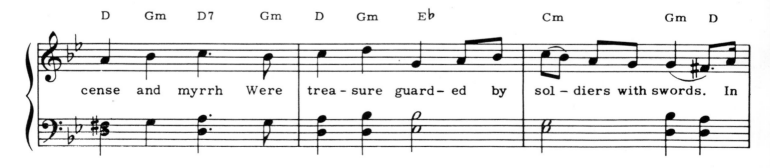

cense and myrrh Were trea-sure guard-ed by sol-diers with swords. In

FROM: INTERNATIONAL CHRISTMAS by Ada Richter
© 1966 Theodore Presser Company
Reprinted By Permission Of The Publisher

car - a-vans marched the three great kings To hon - or Him born the King of kings.

The Cherry-Tree Carol

ANONYMOUS   ANONYMOUS

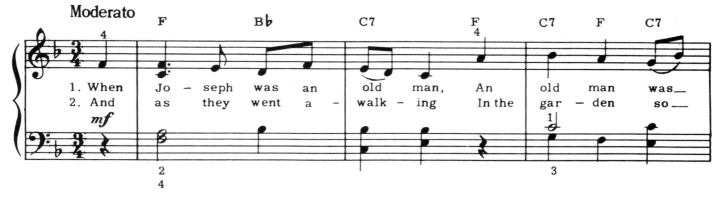

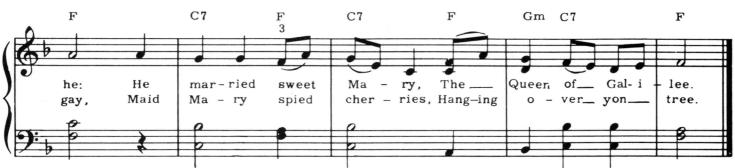

3. Then Mary said to Joseph
   With her sweet lips so mild,
   "Pluck those cherries, Joseph,
   For to give to my Child."

4. And then replied Joseph
   With words so unkind,
   "I will pluck no cherries
   For to give to thy Child."

5. Said Mary to the cherry tree,
   "Bow down to my knee,
   That I may pluck cherries
   By one, two and three."

6. The uppermost sprig then
   Bowed down to her knee,
   "Thus you may see, Joseph,
   These cherries are for me."

7. "O eat your cherries, Mary,
   O eat your cherries now,
   O eat your cherries, Mary,
   That grow upon the bough."

8. As Joseph was a-walking
   He heard angels sing,
   This night there shall be born
   Our heavenly King.

9. "He neither shall be born
   In house nor in hall,
   Nor in the place of Paradise,
   But in an ox-stall.

10. "He shall not be clothed
    In purple nor pall;
    But all in fair linen,
    As wear babies all.

11. "He shall not be rocked
    In silver nor gold,
    But in a wooden cradle
    That rocks on the mould.

12. "He neither shall be christened
    In milk nor in wine,
    But in pure spring-well water
    Fresh sprung from Bethine."

13. Mary took her Baby,
    She dressed Him so sweet,
    She laid Him in a manger
    All there for to sleep.

14. As she stood over Him
    She heard angels sing,
    "Oh, bless our dear Saviour,
    Our heavenly King."

FROM: INTERNATIONAL CHRISTMAS by Ada Richter
© 1966 Theodore Presser Company
Reprinted By Permission Of The Publisher

O Christmas Tree

GERMAN: ANONYMOUS, 1820
ENGLISH: GEORGE W. ANTHONY, 1966

ANONYMOUS, 1799

1. O Christmas tree, O Christmas tree, So green through-out the sea-sons.

So green in sum-mer in the sun, And still as green in win-ter's snow. O

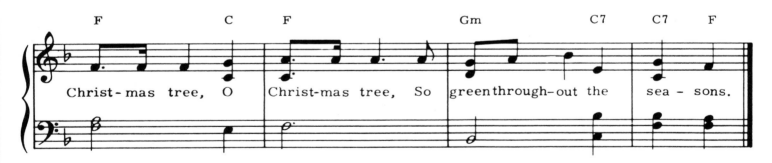

Christ-mas tree, O Christ-mas tree, So green through-out the sea-sons.

2. ‖: O Christmas tree, O Christmas tree,
Your beauty lasts forever. :‖
But most of all at Christmastime
Your boughs so rich bring joy sublime.
O Christmas tree, O Christmas tree,
Your beauty lasts forever.

3. ‖: O Christmas tree, O Christmas tree,
A lesson you can teach us. :‖
You give us hope and constancy,
And strengthen faith, O lovely tree.
O Christmas tree, O Christmas tree,
A lesson you can teach us.

FROM: INTERNATIONAL CHRISTMAS by Ada Richter
© 1966 Theodore Presser Company
Reprinted By Permission Of The Publisher

God Rest You Merry, Gentlemen

ANONYMOUS, c.1770

ANONYMOUS, 1827

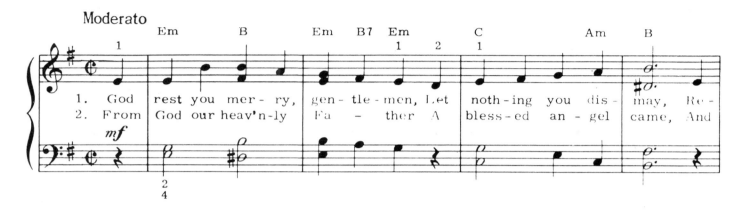

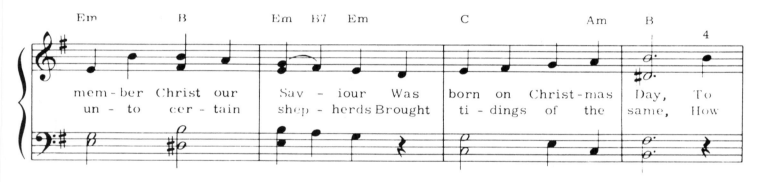

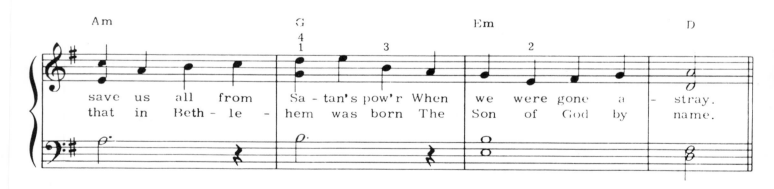

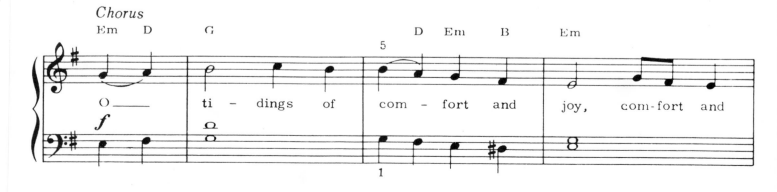

72

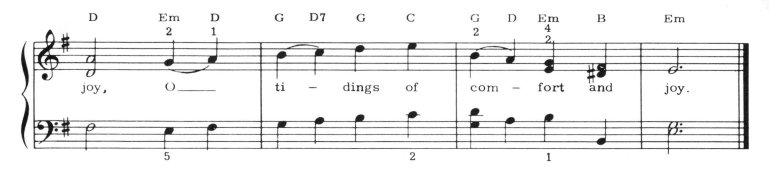

joy, O_____ ti – dings of com – fort and joy.

3. "Fear not," then said the angel,
   "Let nothing you affright,
   This day is born a Saviour
   Of a pure Virgin bright,
   To free all those who trust in Him
   From Satan's pow'r and might."
   Chorus

4. The shepherds at those tidings
   Rejoiced much in mind,
   And left their flocks a-feeding,
   In tempest, storm and wind;
   And went to Bethlehem straightway
   The Son of God to find.
   Chorus

5. And when they came to Bethlehem
   Where our dear Saviour lay,
   They found Him in a manger,
   Where oxen feed on hay;
   His mother Mary kneeling down,
   Unto the Lord did pray.
   Chorus

6. Now to the Lord sing praises,
   All you within this place,
   And with true love and brotherhood
   Each other now embrace;
   This holy tide of Christmas
   All other doth deface.
   Chorus

A Holly Jolly Christmas

JOHNNY MARKS   JOHNNY MARKS

Moderately Bright With A Happy Feeling

Have A HOL - LY JOL - LY CHRIST - MAS, it's the best time of the year.

I don't know if there'll be snow but have a cup of cheer.

Have A HOL - LY JOL - LY CHRIST - MAS, and when you walk down the street

Say hel - lo to friends you know and ev - 'ry - one you

The Boar's Head Carol

ANONYMOUS, 17TH CENTURY

ANONYMOUS, 18TH CENTURY

1. The boar's head in hand bear I, Be - decked with bays and

rose - mar - y; And I pray you my mas - ters mer - ry be; Quot

es - tis in con - vi - vi - o.1) Ca - put a - pri

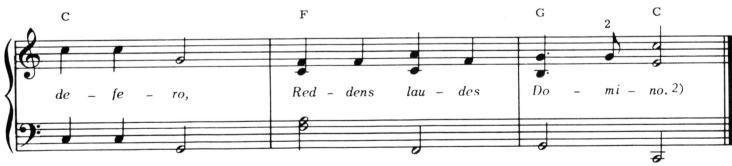

de - fe - ro, Red - dens lau - des Do - mi - no.2)

2. The boar's head I understand
   Is the rarest dish in all this land,
   Which thus bedecked with a garland gay,
   Let us *servire cantico.* 3)
   Chorus

3. Our steward hath provided this
   In honor of the King of bliss,
   Which on this day to be served is,
   In *Reginensi atrio.*4)
   Chorus

1) Everyone who is at this feast.
2) The boar's head I bring, Giving praises to the Lord.

3) Let us serve with a song.
4) In the royal hall.

FROM: INTERNATIONAL CHRISTMAS by Ada Richter
© 1966 Theodore Presser Company
Reprinted By Permission Of The Publisher

Ave Maria

LATIN: ANONYMOUS
ENGLISH: SIR WALTER SCOTT
(1771–1832)

FRANZ SCHUBERT, 1825
(1797–1828)

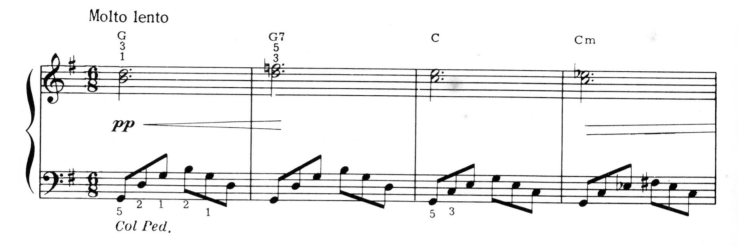

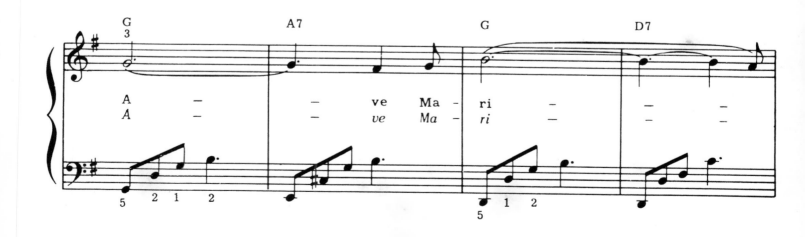

FROM: INTERNATIONAL CHRISTMAS by Ada Richter
© 1966 Theodore Presser Company
Reprinted By Permission Of The Publisher

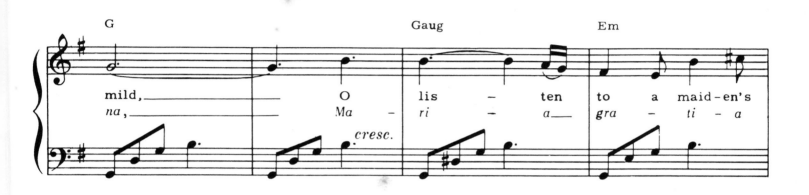

mid _____ de - spair. _____ Safe _____
nus, _____ Do - mi - nus _____ te - cum. _____ Ben - e -

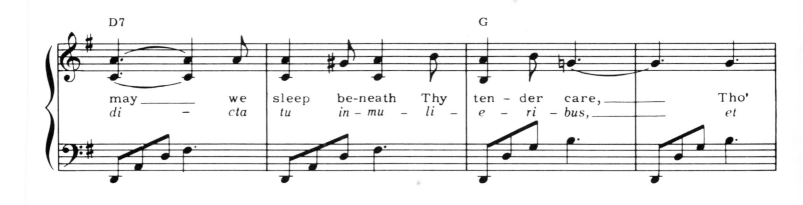

may _____ we sleep be-neath Thy ten - der care, _____ Tho'
di - cta tu in - mu - li - e - ri - bus, _____ et

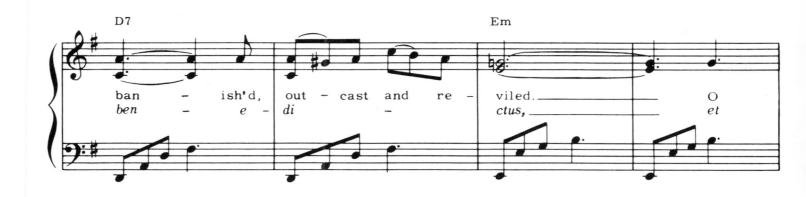

ban - ish'd, out - cast and re - viled. _____ O
ben - e - di - ctus, _____ et

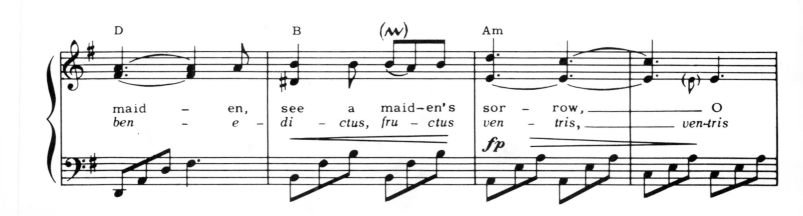

maid - en, see a maid-en's sor - row, _____ O
ben - e - di - ctus, fru - ctus ven - tris, _____ ven-tris

We Wish You A Merry Christmas

ANONYMOUS

ANONYMOUS

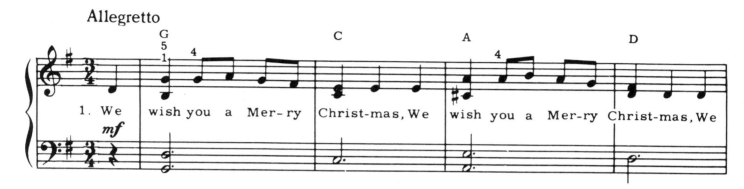

1. We wish you a Mer-ry Christ-mas, We wish you a Mer-ry Christ-mas, We

wish you a Mer – ry Christ-mas, And a Hap – py New Year!

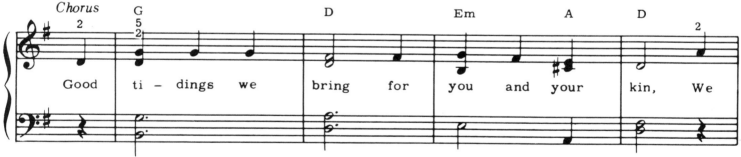

Chorus

Good ti – dings we bring for you and your kin, We

wish you a Mer – ry Christ-mas, And a Hap – py New Year!

2. Oh, bring us some figgy pudding,
   Oh, bring us some figgy pudding,
   Oh, bring us some figgy pudding,
   Now bring some right here!
   Chorus

3. We won't go until we get some,
   We won't go until we get some,
   We won't go until we get some,
   So bring some right here!
   Chorus

FROM: INTERNATIONAL CHRISTMAS by Ada Richter
© 1966 Theodore Presser Company
Reprinted By Permission Of The Publisher

I Heard The Bells On Christmas Day

HENRY LONGFELLOW
ADAPTED BY JOHNNY MARKS

JOHNNY MARKS

1. I HEARD THE BELLS ON CHRIST-MAS DAY, Their old fa-mil-iar car-ols play; And wild and sweet the words re-peat, Of Peace On Earth, Good

2. And in de-spair, I bowed my head, "There is no Peace on Earth," I said, "For Hate is strong and mocks the song Of Peace On Earth, Good

The First Noel

ANONYMOUS, 1833

ANONYMOUS, 1833

Moderato

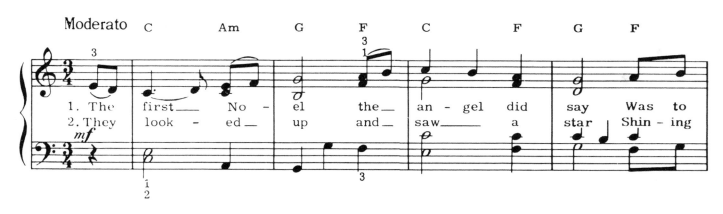

1. The first___ No - el the___ an - gel did say Was to
2. They look - ed___ up and___ saw___ a star Shin - ing

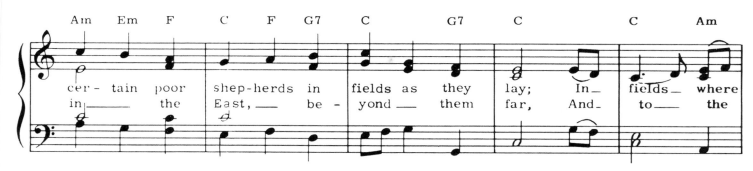

cer - tain poor shep-herds in fields as they lay; In___ fields___ where
in___ the East,___ be - yond___ them far, And___ to___ where the

they lay___ keep-ing their sheep On a cold win - ter's night___ that
earth it___ gave___ great light, And___ so it con - tin - ued both

Chorus

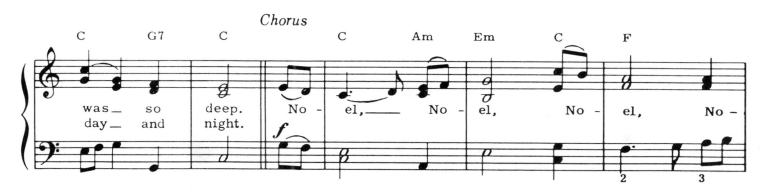

was___ so deep. No - el,___ No - el, No - el, No -
day___ and night.

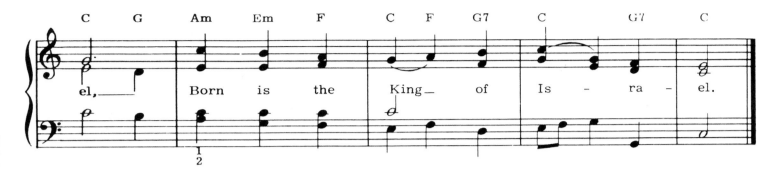

el, _____ | Born is the | King _ of Is - | ra - el.

3. **This star drew nigh to the Northwest,**
   O'er Bethlehem it took its rest,
   And there it did both stop and stay
   Right over the place where Jesus lay.
   Chorus

4. Then enter'd in there Wise-men three,
   Full rev'rently upon their knee,
   And offer'd there in His presence,
   Their gold and myrrh and frankincense.
   Chorus

We Three Kings Of Orient Are

JOHN H. HOPKINS, 1857
(1820–1891)

JOHN H. HOPKINS, 1857
(1820–1891)

1. We three kings of O - ri - ent are; Bear - ing gifts we tra - verse a - far, Field and foun - tain, moor and moun - tain, Fol - low - ing yon - der star. O___ Star of won - der, star of night, Star with roy - al beau - ty bright, West - ward

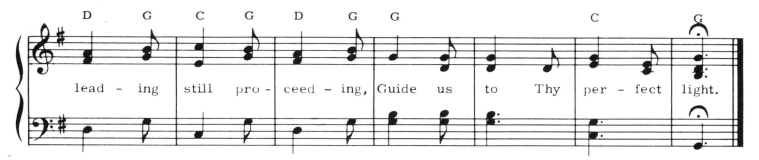

lead - ing still pro - ceed - ing, Guide us to Thy per - fect light.

2. Born a King on Bethlehem's plain,
   Gold I bring, to crown Him again,
   King forever, ceasing never,
   Over us all to reign.
   Chorus

3. Frankincense to offer have I,
   Incense owns a Deity nigh.
   Pray'r and praising, all men raising,
   Worship Him, God most High.
   Chorus

4. Myrrh is mine, its bitter perfume
   Breathes a life of gathering gloom;
   Sorrowing, sighing, bleeding, dying,
   Seal'd in the stone-cold tomb.
   Chorus

5. Glorious now behold Him arise,
   King and God and sacrifice,
   Alleluia, Alleluia;
   Earth to the heav'ns replies.
   Chorus

The Holly And The Ivy

ANONYMOUS, c.1700

ANONYMOUS

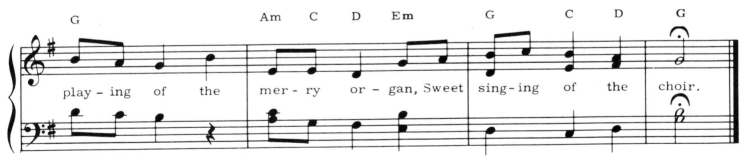

2. The holly bears a blossom,
   As white as the lily flower,
   And Mary bore sweet Jesus Christ,
   To be our sweet Saviour:
   Chorus

3. The holly bears a berry,
   As red as any blood,
   And Mary bore sweet Jesus Christ,
   To do poor sinners good:
   Chorus

4. The holly bears a prickle,
   As sharp as any thorn,
   And Mary bore sweet Jesus Christ,
   On Christmas Day in the morn:
   Chorus

5. The holly bears a bark,
   As bitter as any gall,
   And Mary bore sweet Jesus Christ,
   For to redeem us all:
   Chorus

FROM: INTERNATIONAL CHRISTMAS by Ada Richter
© 1966 Theodore Presser Company
Reprinted By Permission Of The Publisher

93

O Little Town Of Bethlehem

PHILLIPS BROOKS, 1868
(1835–1893)

LEWIS H. REDNER, 1874
(1831–1908)

3. How silently, how silently
   The wondrous gift is given!
   So God imparts to human hearts
   The blessings of His heaven.
   No ear may hear His coming,
   But in the world of sin,
   Where meek souls will receive Him still,
   The dear Christ enters in.

4. O holy Child of Bethlehem!
   Descend to us, we pray;
   Cast out our sin, and enter in,
   Be born in us today.
   We hear the Christmas angels
   The great glad tidings tell;
   O come to us, abide with us,
   Our Lord Immanuel!

FROM: INTERNATIONAL CHRISTMAS by Ada Richter
© 1966 Theodore Presser Company
Reprinted By Permission Of The Publisher

Angels, From The Realms Of Glory

JAMES MONTGOMERY, 1816
(1771–1854)

HENRY SMART, 1867
(1813–1879)

Tempo di Marcia

1. An-gels, from the realms of glo - ry, Wing your flight o'er all the earth;

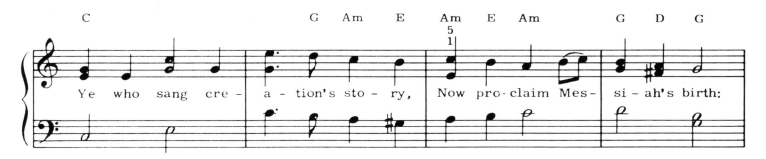

Ye who sang cre - a - tion's sto - ry, Now pro-claim Mes - si – ah's birth:

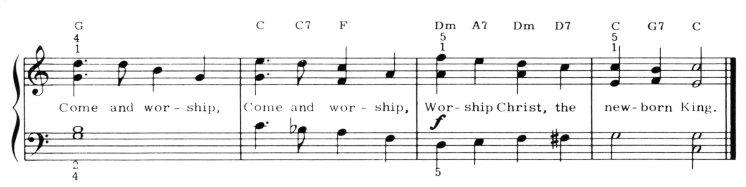

Come and wor - ship, Come and wor - ship, Wor- ship Christ, the new-born King.

2. Shepherds, in the field abiding,
   Watching o'er your flocks by night,
   God with man is now residing;
   Yonder shines the infant Light:
   Come and worship,
   Come and worship,
   Worship Christ, the new-born King.

3. Sages, leave your contemplations,
   Brighter visions beam afar;
   Seek the great Desire of nations;
   Ye have seen His natal star:
   Come and worship,
   Come and worship,
   Worship Christ, the new-born King.

4. Saints, before the altar bending,
   Watching long in hope and fear,
   Suddenly the Lord, descending,
   In His temple shall appear:
   Come and worship,
   Come and worship,
   Worship Christ, the new-born King.

FROM: INTERNATIONAL CHRISTMAS by Ada Richter
© 1966 Theodore Presser Company
Reprinted By Permission Of The Publisher

Auld Lang Syne

1ST VERSE, ANONYMOUS
2ND VERSE, ROBERT BURNS, c.1796
(1759–1796)

ANONYMOUS, c.1792

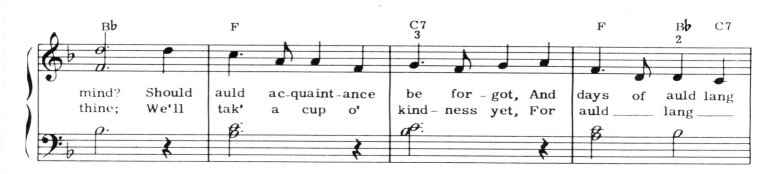

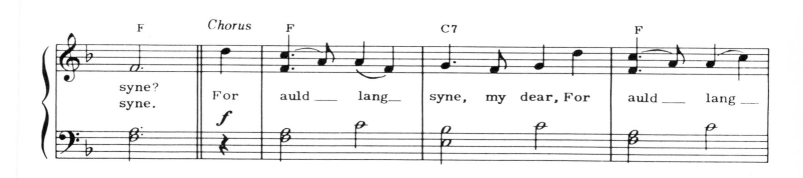

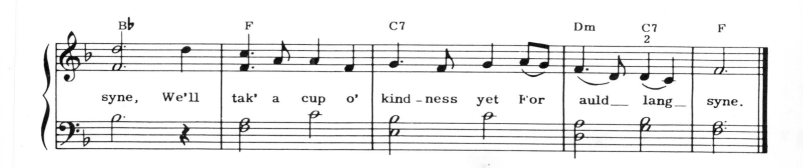